The Satchmo' Suite

THE SATCHMO' SUITE

Hans Böggild & Doug Innis

Talonbooks

Talonbooks
P.O. Box 2076, Vancouver, British Columbia, Canada V6B 3S3
www.talonbooks.com

Typeset in New Baskerville and printed and bound in Canada.
Printed on 100% post-consumer recycled paper.

First Printing: 2010

The publisher gratefully acknowledges the financial support of the
Canada Council for the Arts; the Government of Canada through the
Book Publishing Industry Development Program; and the Province of
British Columbia through the British Columbia Arts Council and the
Book Publishing Tax Credit for our publishing activities.

Library and Archives Canada Cataloguing in Publication

Böggild, Hans, 1956–
    The Satchmo' suite / Hans Böggild & Doug Innis.

A play.
ISBN 978-0-88922-648-7

    I. Innis, Doug, 1950– II. Title.

PS8603.O354S27 2010   C812'.6   C2010-902278-5

Play the lick. Play the riff. Play your truth.

The first version of *The Satchmo' Suite* was a one-person show. Commissioned by Mulgrave Road Theatre, it premiered in 1995, and toured Nova Scotia with the following cast:

HUBERT CLEMENTS / LOUIS ARMSTRONG: Doug Innis
PIANO PLAYER: Don Coward
Director: Hans Böggild
Set and Lighting Designer: Philip Cygan
Stage Manager: Selena Landon
Assistant Stage Manager: Allison Spearin
Dramaturge: Paul Ledoux
Commissioned by Allena MacDonald

Mulgrave Road Theatre remounted the play in 1996. Doug Innis reprised his dual roles, Emmy Alcorn directed the production, and the PIANO PLAYER was Kim Dunn.

In 2004, Böggild and Innis rewrote the piece to involve an ensemble cast of five. They also wrote nine original jazz songs and three instrumental compositions so that the play is a suite in twelve movements. The new and current version premiered at Eastern Front Theatre in March 2005 with the following cast:

HUBERT CLEMENTS: Andrew Moodie
LOUIS ARMSTRONG: Jeremiah Sparks
PIANO PLAYER: Paul Simons
CELLO PLAYER: Colin Matthews
TRUMPET PLAYER: Mike Cowie
Director: Hans Böggild

Set and Costume Designer: Denyse Karn
Lighting Designer: Leigh Ann Vardy
Stage Manager: Hilary Graham
Assistant Director: Louise Renault
Production Manager: Louisa Adamson

In 2006, Eastern Front Theatre remounted the play at Neptune Studio Theatre. It was then featured at the Magnetic North Theatre Festival. In the fall of 2006, the play was part of the Saidye Bronfman Centre for the Arts (now Segal Centre for Performing Arts) theatrical season in Montreal. In 2008, the play went on a Western Canada tour with three season runs at Vancouver East Cultural Centre, Western Canada Theatre in Kamloops, and the Manitoba Theatre Centre in Winnipeg. Other musicians featured in these subsequent productions were: John Gilbert (Piano), Rick Waychesco (Trumpet), Bill Mahar (Trumpet), and Derry Byrne (Trumpet).

The authors would like to acknowledge the support of Canadian Heritage, The Canada Council for the Arts, and The Nova Scotia Department of Tourism, Culture and Heritage for their support of initial and subsequent productions of *The Satchmo' Suite*.

Characters

HUBERT CLEMENTS: *Mid- to late forties. A modern-day black classical cellist. He's intellectual— All "head."*

LOUIS ARMSTRONG: *At mid-career, timeless, the man we all know as "The Father of Jazz." He's intuitive— All "heart."*

If possible, the actors should bear resemblance to each other. In any case, both of them wear tuxedos.

The play also requires three musicians:

THE PIANO PLAYER

THE CLASSICAL CELLIST

THE TRUMPET PLAYER

The musicians, who are visible on stage, also wear tuxedos.

The action takes place in the hotel room where
HUBERT CLEMENTS presently stays while on tour with
a classical symphony. There's a lonely anonymous
feeling to this room. It has a certain "no man's land"
atmosphere. As well as being a real hotel room, in
another sense it's the "hotel room of the mind"— A
place that is not home, but where home is constantly
missed. There are no walls in this hotel room. They are
defined by the placement of furniture and props. There
is a bed, two chairs, and a small bedside table with a
telephone on it. In the right corner of the room, there is
a music stand with music on it. Up right, there is a
sink/bathroom area with an invisible mirror through
which the characters can look at themselves and each
other while being clearly visible to the audience. The
play uses empty spaces as acting areas for various
scenes that happen in other places and at other times.

There are three levels to the set: the inner hotel room
mentioned above is defined by a central raked square
platform, the outer level is defined by another square
raked platform holding the inner room platform within
it, and the ground level of the stage itself defines
several downstage playing areas. The lighting must
accommodate fluid mood and scene changes, and is
just as vital as the set.

Down right at ground level, there's an area for the
CLASSICAL CELLIST. The CELLIST plays the cello
passages that HUBERT practises during the play.

*Up left at ground level, there is a piano where the
PIANO PLAYER sits throughout the play. He will
provide classical and jazz musical accompaniment as
necessary, as well as mood music throughout.*

*Down left at ground level, there's an area for the
TRUMPET PLAYER, who will play all the trumpet
passages that LOUIS plays during the action.*

*All of the musicians are visible throughout, but mostly
in the shadows ...*

*In the darkness we hear the cello playing J.S. Bach's
Prelude Suite #1, Prelude #1, from "Six Suites for Solo
Cello."*

*A tight thin spotlight fades in on the CELLIST's hands
and arms, on the bow and strings, as the piece
progresses ...*

*Another tight thin spotlight picks out the hands and
arms of HUBERT CLEMENTS, a black man in his mid-
forties sitting at a music stand in the inner hotel room.
He mimes playing the cello piece along with the
CELLIST. HUBERT has no cello or bow, but his miming
is exact, using the same bowing as the CELLIST.
HUBERT concentrates intensely on the sheet music in
front of him, "playing it" with virtuosity ...*

*The spotlight on HUBERT widens and brightens as the
spotlight on the CELLIST (who continues playing
under) fades down ...*

*HUBERT wears an undershirt, dress pants, and a pair
of suspenders that presently hang at the sides of his
pants.*

*The music is hauntingly beautiful, and HUBERT is
visibly moved by his own playing. He reaches a
particularly crucial point near the end of the piece and
messes up the passage. He stops playing ... (CELLO
out.)*

HUBERT stamps his foot in frustration ...

The PIANO PLAYER plays the single notes of the just blown passage, while simultaneously, HUBERT concentrates intensely on the score in front of him …

HUBERT and the CELLIST replay the Bach passage. They mess it up again. HUBERT takes a breath …

The PIANO plays a slow series of lonely chords under the following …

HUBERT gets up from his chair. With one fluid movement he puts on his dress shirt and vest, which wait for him on the back of a nearby chair. He goes to the bathroom area and buttons his shirt in the mirror, occasionally glancing back towards the music on his music stand.

HUBERT crosses towards his music stand as the PIANO plays the single notes of the Bach passage. HUBERT buttons the final buttons on his shirt in time with the music.

The PIANO plays another lonely chord …

HUBERT makes a decision. He crosses to the phone and dials an eleven-digit number. He looks disappointed for a second as he listens to something on the other end of the line. When he's heard the beep …

HUBERT

(*into phone*) Rosie? … It's me, Hubert … Would you phone me back? …

I know you're standing there looking at the call display.

I need to talk to you …

> *He's about to hang up, but instead decides to wander carrying the phone …*

14

HUBERT

(*into phone*) Look, we're going to be together, or we're not. Your call ... No, look Rosie, I want us to stay together, I L ...

> *HUBERT wants to say he loves her, but he can't right now ...*

HUBERT

(*deep breath*) I've had an extremely challenging day. This morning, at rehearsal, I'm informed that the guest soloist has "taken ill." (*laugh*) Taken ill— The fool. He was bitten by his pet Angora bunny. "Here's Mr. Fluffy, my travelling companion! Say hello, little man! Ow! My finger!" ... It would be a great laugh Rosie, except I've been asked to fill in. They want me to play the first Bach suite for solo cello in honour of Bach's birthday! Wonderful! I've played it for twenty years! A million times! It's like one of those forties movies where the stand-in goes on for the star, except ...

> *HUBERT crosses back to his music stand and sits on his chair ...*

HUBERT

(*into phone*) When my illustrious conductor Volkovsky asks me to play the piece in rehearsal, I give it everything it needs, Rosie, everything! ... Until the tenth note of the twenty-fourth measure— My God, my fingers develop a mind of their own! Time, phrasing, emotional content— It all goes out the window, and I'm fudging it! I keep going, Rosie, but I'm fudging it! And everybody knows!

> *HUBERT picks up a pencil and taps it against his music stand through the next line ...*

HUBERT

> (*into phone*) So Volkovsky taps his baton on his podium, stopping me in the middle of the piece. I look up at him and hear ...

> *HUBERT says the next line in a Viennese accent ...*

HUBERT

> (*into phone*) "Mr. Clements! This is not an improvisation! This is not a jam! This is not even marmalade! It is Bach! If you want so badly to improvise, why don't you join Louis Armstrong's band! After all, you and Satchmo' have so much in common!"

> *Beat ... HUBERT's dignity is hurt ... He stands up ...*

HUBERT

> (*into phone*) There I am, dangling in the wind in front of the whole orchestra. None of them will look at me. I hung on to my dignity ... Well, at least I, barely, got through the rest of the piece.

> *HUBERT crosses left, away from the music stand ...*

HUBERT

> (*into phone*) ... Of all the people for that Boehunk to compare me to! Satchmo'. He calls me Satchmo'.

> *HUBERT crosses to where a "window" might be in the hotel room ...*

HUBERT

> (*into phone*) I'm performing the suite tonight ... If I misquote that line, I might just hurl myself out of this hotel window and finally deal with the eternal conundrum. Rosie, get back to me. I don't even know what town I'm in. This tour is driving me crazy. Call the number on the call display. I don't even know what room I'm in. I'm in some hotel

16

room of the mind somewhere ... Say hi to the boys
for me.

*HUBERT hangs up. He crosses back to his music stand,
and picks up his invisible cello ...*

HUBERT

Okay I've got to break down this passage
systematically ...

*HUBERT looks at the sheet music, as the PIANO plays
the single notes of the Bach passage. HUBERT picks up
his "bow," readies it on the "strings," and tries the
Bach passage again. He flubs it again. In need of
comfort, he sits back in his chair, and rubs his temples.*

HUBERT

Herr Bach, you are a sadist ...

He gets up, and puts on his tuxedo jacket ...

HUBERT

If I can't play that phrase, at least I'm going to look
like I can ...

*He crosses to the bathroom area and looks in the mirror
through the following ...*

HUBERT

(*playfully*) Satchmo' ... Satchmo' ... Miles Davis? I
could manage that. Freddie Hubbard? A
gentleman. Charles Mingus? A genius. But no—
He calls me SATCHMO'!

*With this last "SATCHMO'" he's playfully added just a
touch of the stereotype Louis Armstrong voice and grin.
He does a musical phrase in Louis Armstrong style
scat ...*

HUBERT

Da boo da bee, dee da boo day ...

He takes a beat, then says in his own voice ...

HUBERT

A man who "Uncle Tommed" his way through lyrics
he wanted everyone to think he was too dumb to
remember.

> *Looking in the mirror, HUBERT sings another scat
> line ...*

HUBERT

Da bo day bo da da de day splot splat splat zot ...

> *He looks back towards his music stand, and says
> politely what he wishes he'd said to his conductor ...*

HUBERT

Herr Volkovsky. Maestro. I am not the Uncle Tom
of this orchestra, no matter how you would have it.

> *He turns back to the mirror and yells in frustration ...*

HUBERT

Satchmo'. SATCHMO'!!!

> *LOUIS ARMSTRONG appears suddenly, looking back at
> HUBERT from the other side of the mirror.*

HUBERT

The rolling of the eyes.

> *HUBERT rolls his eyes Louis style, as LOUIS does ex-
> actly the same, a mirror image of HUBERT ...*

HUBERT

The ivory grin.

> *HUBERT and LOUIS mug the famous Louis Armstrong
> grin at each other, and hold it for a second on each
> side of the mirror ...*

HUBERT

Them shuffling "feets."

> *HUBERT and LOUIS do an identical tomming walk
> towards each other and the invisible edge of the mirror.*

HUBERT moves his hands around and makes expressions into the mirror as LOUIS mirrors HUBERT's movements exactly.

Finally, LOUIS breaks this with a wave of his hand, and begins to speak directly to HUBERT ...

LOUIS

Come on Hubert, what's with all this minor key obbligato? (*laughs*) You used to love my pearlies, peepers, and poise. Now you don't like my teeth, or my eyes, or my walk. You don't even like my good name. Uncle Tom, you call me!

HUBERT

That's what you are, Satchmo'.

LOUIS

I ain't an Uncle Tom— Hell I don't even own a cabin.

HUBERT

You never had any dignity!

LOUIS

I've got my dignity! And I earned it! Gettin' our music to the people. I had new ideas, a new approach. I opened doors that had never opened for a black man before. And once I opened them doors, they stayed open!

HUBERT

You didn't open every door Louis, and many of them are still locked up tight.

LOUIS

Well what you want Pops to do boy, walk on water?

19

HUBERT

You could have set some new ground rules on your way through. Created a positive image, instead of acting like a circus clown.

LOUIS

Clown! Now that does pain me Hubert. It's not the fact you don't like my act, it's the hatred I'm hearin' in your upper register. Hatin' somebody is just a way of blamin' other people for your own shortcomings.

HUBERT

(*smiles*) I'm a perfectly acceptable human being— I have no shortcomings.

LOUIS

Feelin' a little insecure about something Hubert? ... Worried maybe tonight you'll be the cat in the red rubber nose?

LOUIS crosses downstage, still on the outer level, and as if reaching through the wall, he grabs the sheet music from HUBERT's music stand ...

HUBERT crosses downstage in the inner room and snatches the sheet music back from LOUIS ...

HUBERT

Give me that! You can't read music anyway!

LOUIS snatches the sheet music back from HUBERT ...

LOUIS

Eubie, I read music so well, cats like you think I'm just jammin'!

Carrying the music, LOUIS walks downstage left until he gets to the TRUMPET PLAYER at ground level.

LOUIS

    Let's see here … Your trouble is right here at the tenth note of the twenty-fourth measure.

        LOUIS mimes playing the Bach line on his "trumpet," in a jazz style. (Simultaneously the TRUMPET PLAYER plays the passage on the trumpet.)

LOUIS

    There's nothin' to that. What's your problem man?

HUBERT

    The way you just played that would be wonderful if Bach wrote it as a swing tune, but it's not!

LOUIS

    It don't mean a thing if it ain't got that swing!

        LOUIS steps back onto the outer level, getting closer again to HUBERT who's still in the inner room …

HUBERT

    The last I heard, Johann Sebastian never played on a riverboat steamer!

LOUIS

    Of course he didn't! Steamers weren't invented yet. But if he had been playin' on a steamer, he would have swung that line man!

HUBERT

    That's ridiculous! That would be like mixing Bartók with Mahler!

LOUIS

    But don't forget old Fats Waller!

        Through the "wall," HUBERT grabs the sheet music back from LOUIS and displays it for him …

HUBERT

    This is Bach! You can't just apply any style to Bach!

LOUIS

Why not? I just did!

HUBERT arranges his music back on his music stand …

HUBERT

There are very strict rules to playing Bach's music!

LOUIS

Maybe those rules are what's gettin' in the way of you playin' it!

HUBERT

What would you know about it?

LOUIS

Well, I know, for instance, that Duke Ellington borrowed a lot of chords from Debussy and Ravel. And congruously, old Dvořák used a lot of black gospel and jazz in his thing!

HUBERT

And your point is?

LOUIS

The point is Hubert that there are only two kinds of music!

HUBERT

Oh? And what would they be Louis?

LOUIS

Well, there's good music, and there's bad music!

HUBERT walks back to his side of the mirror through the following line …

HUBERT

Of course! You would come up with a wonderfully simple theory like that! Completely overlooking the complexities of style in the progression of the history of Western art music!

*LOUIS arrives back at his side of the mirror at exactly
the same time, and stares back at HUBERT ...*

LOUIS

Simplicity is the key man! Your trouble is you're
just all too complex!

HUBERT

How dare you come in here and patronize me like
this!

LOUIS

Old Pops just tryin' to help so you won't look like a
clown tonight.

HUBERT

Clown! You take the cake in the clown department.
Satchmo', the movie star. You're standing knee-
high in soap suds wearing a leopard-skin loincloth
singing (*mockingly*) "That's why they calls me
shines!" There's no way I'm going to top that
Louis. No sir. You are the clown!

*The PIANO backs LOUIS up on the song "Start a New
Day."*

LOUIS

(*singing*) You think you're right
Where I am concerned
But there's a thing or two
You've got to learn
You feel better when you're
Putting me down
Maybe it's you who's the clown

*HUBERT crosses downstage to his music stand and
sits, and LOUIS crosses downstage on the outer level,
following him ...*

23

LOUIS

> (*singing*) You don't feel good about yourself
> You're always blaming someone else
> You like to look down on everyone you see
>
> (*spoken:*) Includin' me ...
>
> You're takin' yourself too seriously
> You're in love with misery
> You like to complain and to you that's fun!
>
>> *HUBERT moans loudly and covers his eyes with his hands ...*
>>
>> (*Bridge, right off HUBERT's moan ...*)

LOUIS

> (*singing*) You moan and moan and moan and moan,
> And then you moan some more
> What can you say about a cat like you
> That hasn't been said before?
>
>> *TRUMPET solo— (LOUIS mimes as the TRUMPET PLAYER plays ...)*
>>
>> *HUBERT moans loudly again ...*

LOUIS

> (*singing*) You moan and moan and moan and moan,
> And then you moan some more
> What can I say about a cat like you
> That hasn't been said before?
>
>> *LOUIS pushes towards the end of the tune ...*

LOUIS

> (*singing*) Listen friend, it's not the end
> Of this your sad sad story
> Take a glance at a second chance
> To reach some kind of glory

It's time to find a new way

> *TRUMPET shot— (LOUIS mimes)*

It's time to start a new day

> *TRUMPET shot— (LOUIS mimes)*

It's time to be on your way

> *TRUMPET shot— (LOUIS mimes)*

And start a brand new story!

LOUIS

(*scats*) Zo zo zo Zop! De so so so zop!
Oh YEAH!!! …

> *LOUIS bows then mops the sweat off his forehead with a large white handkerchief.*

> *HUBERT crosses back into the bathroom, followed by LOUIS who meets him back on the other side of the mirror.*

HUBERT

Thank you Louis. Thank you from the bottom of my heart. It's been a slice having this talk with you … Goodbye.

> *HUBERT washes his face in the basin, and dries his face with a towel. Looking up into the mirror, he's surprised to see that LOUIS still stands there looking back at him …*

LOUIS

Hold on now Hubert, I ain't going nowhere. You call me all kinds of nasty things to make yourself feel better, and expect me to just lie down and take it? … I don't think so!

> *HUBERT starts tying his bow tie in the mirror, as LOUIS glances towards HUBERT's music stand.*

LOUIS

Nah— Truth is Hubert, I kinda likes you. I always
was a sucker for a good musician. And you are a
mellow fellow on that there violoncello!

HUBERT

Oh how kind of you! Thank you so very much!
Now I've had enough— Get out of here.

> *HUBERT messes up tying his bow tie, and abandons
> the exercise in frustration …*

LOUIS

Yeah, I loves the way you bow that cello! But
Hubert baby, you gotta learn to bow this tie! You
got to give some class to your sash! If you'll permit
me, I'll show you how it's done!

> *LOUIS lunges right through the mirror to HUBERT on
> the other side, and perfectly ties HUBERT's bow tie for
> him over the next lines …*

LOUIS

Here, let me give you a hand. (*Scats while tying, then
finishes …*) Now Eubie's back in town. Ta, da!!
There it is!

HUBERT

(*dryly*) Ta. Da.

LOUIS

Now at least you look like you might play that Bach
lick!

HUBERT

Gee Louis, thanks for the vote of confidence.

> *LOUIS enters the inner hotel room through the invisible
> wall. He looks around the room, then to HUBERT …*

LOUIS

Okay Hubert. Let's get down to it. You're gettin' all
bent out of shape over a little insult.

HUBERT

It is not a "little" insult— It's a fully formed racially
motivated slap in the face!

LOUIS

Oh yeah ... It must be hell to be compared to me,
huh, huh ...

HUBERT

I'm so sorry to hurt your feelings and bruise your
enormous ego Louis, but it is.

LOUIS

Might as well compare you to the devil himself!
Huh, huh ... Now what do you suppose that old
rascal Volkovsky is up to?

HUBERT

He's trying to destroy my confidence!

LOUIS

Whatever he said to you, was only to make you feel
like you're feelin' now. The more you let it
straighten your hair, the more he's gonna win.

HUBERT

I know that! My entire career is on the line ...

LOUIS

Then you best put your ego on hold, and "Do the
Do" my friend. By way of example I will now deliver
a short but entertainin' "anecdote"— Love that
word, it means a funny story *and* a cure for poison.

*LOUIS "plays" a flashy TRUMPET lick, sits down on a
chair, then launches into a story ...*

27

LOUIS

My first recording session, I'm blowin' my horn
like mad! ...

TRUMPET shot— Even flashier ...

LOUIS

I'm wild! I'm flashy! ...

TRUMPET shot— A stab ...

LOUIS

I'm cookin'! ...

*TRUMPET shot— A final shot and louder than the
rest ...*

LOUIS

When the engineer yells out at me, "Hey you!
You're playing too loud! Move back!" Now I'm
mad! Who's this cat to tell *me* where I should be? I
feel like storming out of there! So I pick up my
horn! I pick up my music stand! ... (*beat*) And I
move my chair back ten feet ...

*LOUIS moves his chair back and flashes his pearly
whites.*

HUBERT

Just what are you telling me to do Louis?— Go sit
at the back of the bus?

LOUIS

Hey, I didn't think we was talkin' buses, I thought
we was talkin' a cookin' classical combo!

HUBERT

We are "talkin'" a good orchestra! The best I've
ever played with. If I blow this piece tonight I'm
going to lose my chair. Once you lose your chair,
you never get it back.

LOUIS

My chair! Your chair! Who cares? The question is
what was it that made you wanna be a musician in
the first place?

Good question ... HUBERT remembers ...

HUBERT

... I've played my instrument since I was a knock-
kneed kid from Nova Scotia.

LOUIS

Yeah! ...

HUBERT

From the moment I got a *sound* out of it, I was
hooked, like a fish, on the end of a line.

LOUIS

Yes sir! Tell it!

*HUBERT looks at the score of the Bach piece on the
music stand, as he continues ...*

HUBERT

I entered competitions— I won some, I lost some. I
received scholarships and I have mastered this
instrument. And now, I'm first chair! Top of the
metaphoric musical food chain!

LOUIS

Yeah, you's the king fish all right!

HUBERT

But all this fish wants is to get off that line, swim off
someplace, and die.

LOUIS

You've worked too hard just to swim off man ...
You're the top! You're like the tower of Pisa! Maybe
you're leanin' a little, but just hang in there! Hold
your ground!

HUBERT

Holding this job should have nothing to do with whether I can tie a bow tie Louis. But maybe it does.

LOUIS

Oh man …

HUBERT

And it should have nothing to do with how bright my teeth are Louis, but maybe it does … Just because my colour is a little "shady"?

LOUIS

Forget colour! Now what do you wanna say to your Mr. Volkovsky?

HUBERT

(*Viennese accent*) Maestro, it's not going to vurk. (*in his own voice*) I am playing tonight!

LOUIS

Bingo!! Now play it!

HUBERT looks defiantly at the sheet music in front of him. The PIANO plays the one-note version of the cello passage, as HUBERT concentrates on the sheet music.

HUBERT puts his "bow" on the strings. He plays the passage. He messes it up again. In frustration, he "bows" three angry stabs on the strings …

LOUIS

Hubert, you're more backed up than a doo rag stuck in a toilet bowl! Let it out! Let it all out!!! You got to learn how to laugh at life! Like the man says, it's a cabaret!

HUBERT rises and crosses to the "window" …

HUBERT

I'd love to come to the cabaret, old chum, but Herr Goebbels is booking the pit band, and I've got no control over the politics of my situation.

LOUIS joins HUBERT at the "window" …

LOUIS

Hubert, what are you talkin' about? You's the one in the driver's seat. Now you may think I was an Uncle Tom, but I was always in the driver's seat. Had to be! Or they woulda shot me down faster than a gangster on Valentine's Day.

The PIANO starts vamping on the tune of "Scoundrel" …

LOUIS crosses down to the lower level, next to the TRUMPET PLAYER and the PIANO PLAYER …

LOUIS

Yeah … Tell you about it … I'm playin' Chicago … Man we're wailin'! I'm talkin' hot! I'm just comin' down off my solo …

LOUIS "plays" the ending of a TRUMPET solo with the piano. PIANO keeps vamping the tune under the following …

LOUIS

… When I notice this mean lookin' white cat come in the back entrance of the club. And this cat smiles at me. I'm thinkin', do I know this cat?— When up comes my verse …

LOUIS sings with the piano …

LOUIS

(*singing*) I knew you were a scoundrel when you walked in
I knew you were a scoundrel when you walked in

31

You finished off my whiskey
Then you drank up all my gin
I knew you were a scoundrel when you walked in!

> *LOUIS notices something in the crowd. PIANO*
> *under ...*

LOUIS

(*picking up story*) Now, this cat starts gesturing like
this, like he wants to talk to me right now. I figure,
maybe I better listen to this cat's jive.

> *LOUIS turns to the PIANO PLAYER ...*

LOUIS

So I says, "Hey, Father Earl, take a solo." And I
walks to this cat's table, and sits down.

> *The PIANO PLAYER plays a short flourish on the*
> *vamp, as LOUIS moves to a chair and sits down. The*
> *PIANO vamps under ...*

LOUIS

And this cat says he wants me and my band in New
York City tomorrow night at some club. I got a
three-week gig right here in Chicago, so I tell him,
"Thank you, but I don't plan no travelin'."

> *The PIANO music cuts out abruptly.*

LOUIS

This cat looks at me, smiles, opens his lapel, and
he's packin' the biggest forty-five I've ever seen. He
pulls it out. He cocks it, puts it under the table, and
points it right at my short and curlies!

> *LOUIS demonstrates this ...*

LOUIS

... And smiles real broad— Like he's imitatin' me,
you know. So I says to him, "A little trip to New

York tomorrow might be just what the doctor
ordered."

> *The PIANO comes back in on the vamp again ...*

LOUIS

I stand up and shake his hand, "Yes sir, tomorrow
night— Me and you! Broadway!" And make my way
back to the bandstand. I knows what I'm really
gonna do. Pack up my band, check out of the
hotel, and book that job I've been puttin' off over
in Europe. So, when I'm finally back on stage ...

> *LOUIS looks towards where the gangster might be on
> stage ...*

LOUIS

... and my verse is comin up, I points down at Mr.
Forty-five and says, "Listen up baby, this one's for
you!" And I sings ...

LOUIS

(*singing*) I'll be pleased as punch when they lay you
six feet deep
I'll be tickled pink when they put you down to
sleep
I'll be livin' my life emancipated
While the devil's got you incarcerated!
I knew you were a scoundrel when you walked in!

LOUIS

(*singing*) I knew you'd be some trouble when you
got here
I knew you'd be a nasty wretch you dog
I brought you home for dinner
And you groped my wife you sinner
I knew you'd be some trouble when you got here!

> *LOUIS goes for the final verse, with some dancing
> too ...*

LOUIS

(*singing*) I knew you were a scoundrel when you
walked in
I knew you were a scoundrel when you walked in
If you fool around here too often
I'll put you in your coffin
I knew you were a scoundrel when you walked in!

> *LOUIS finishes it with a sizzling TRUMPET ending.*

LOUIS

Oh yeah!

> *LOUIS bows then mops his brow with his large white
> handkerchief. He joins HUBERT back up in the inner
> hotel room.*

HUBERT

That's a marvelous "anecdote," Louis. But basically
you ran away.

LOUIS

I didn't run away, I decided to go to Europe, 'cause
I was in the driver's seat of my car!

> *HUBERT picks up a picture of his family from the
> bedside table …*

HUBERT

Louis. I have a wife who's thinking of leaving me,
and two small children who I love. They depend on
me. I can't run away.

> *LOUIS takes the family picture from HUBERT …*

LOUIS

'Course you can't. That's what I meant. (*looking at
the picture*)

This is one beautiful black woman Hubert. I always
used to say, "The blacker the berry, the sweeter the
juice." Mmmm Mmmm!

34

HUBERT snatches the picture back from LOUIS …

HUBERT

She's *my* wife. And I don't know anything about black berries.

LOUIS takes the picture back from HUBERT …

LOUIS

Hey, now don't go gettin' offended. Your Rosie here looks like a younger version of my mother.

HUBERT snatches the picture back from LOUIS …

HUBERT

Well she's not your mother. And as far as colour is concerned, my mother is a white woman. (*Puts picture down.*) And you want to know something else? She …

HUBERT holds himself back, then …

LOUIS

Come on Eubie, spit it out! What's the matter? What are *you* running away from?

HUBERT

You wouldn't understand.

LOUIS

Try me!

HUBERT

This whole conversation is absurd. We come from totally different planets. So let's call the whole thing off.

LOUIS

Love that tune!

HUBERT, suddenly terrified, moves to his cello. LOUIS follows …

HUBERT

What am I doing?! I don't have time for this. I'm
performing tonight!

> *HUBERT picks up his "bow." He puts the hair to the
> strings, as the PIANO plays the single notes of the Bach
> passage ... He's just about to play the Bach passage,
> but he doesn't. He puts his "bow" down without
> playing a note.*

HUBERT

Maybe I should get a real job. Like digging ditches.
A job demanding simple skills and requiring no
distasteful political compromises— A hole to dig,
and that's it.

> *Silence. HUBERT gets a glass of water.*

HUBERT

What do you think Louis?

LOUIS

About what?

HUBERT

About me, digging ditches.

LOUIS

Why? You think there's something wrong with that?

HUBERT

No, no, no ... I'm simply asking what you think
about me being a "ditch-digging fellow," with his
noble shovel ...

LOUIS

You mean instead of holdin' your violoncello?

HUBERT

Yes. What do you think?

> *LOUIS ignores the question, shaking his head ...*

36

LOUIS

Oh get off it Eubie ...

HUBERT

Aren't you going to tell me that it'll wreck my
fingers, and ruin my playing? That I'm too good a
player to be digging ditches, or something? Give
me something! Please ...

LOUIS

Okay Hubert, I'll try ... Now, it's like this ... I've
worked in whorehouses, palaces, great theatres of
the world. I've lunched with presidents and royalty.
I even traded licks with the Pope. And, you know,
I've *dug* ditches.

HUBERT

Of course you have ...

LOUIS

And let me tell you. The same politics I learned in
all those highfalutin' places, were right down there
in those ditches I was diggin' ... You'll always find
someone who thinks they have a bigger shovel than
you. There'll always be someone wantin' your
shovel 'cause they figure theirs is too small. And
finally, there'll always be someone who just doesn't
like the way you *hold* your shovel. I mean man,
sometimes you just can't win. But you're gonna
lose for sure, if you don't try ...

Beat.

HUBERT

Boys *try* Louis, men *do.*

LOUIS

That's right! So be a man! Get to the bottom of
what's really buggin' you.

HUBERT
I'm trying to forget what's "buggin' me."

LOUIS
Hey, you can't forget daddy. Once you know the
score, it's committed to the old memory banks.
The trick is playin' it Hubert, being able to express
it. Come on Hubert, what you hidin' under that
stern classical exterior of yours? You got my interest
all piqued. Who are you? What are you all about?

Beat. HUBERT remembers …

HUBERT
Okay … For a while, my mother and I lived with
her parents … In Sydney, Nova Scotia …

LOUIS
So, you're living with your grandparents?

HUBERT
Yes. My grandparents … They were always sick. So
there were never any picnics or outings to the
park …

HUBERT laughs softly, remembering something.

HUBERT
Except once …

*PIANO hits single notes as HUBERT steps into the outer
level … The musicians play the instrumental tune
"The Park Is Amber" under …*

LOUIS
Where are you?

Lighting changes to take us to the following …

HUBERT
Wentworth Park … There's a pond with geese,
soon to fly south. Brave sun worshippers catch the
last rays of a Nova Scotian Indian summer.

HUBERT is drawn further into the memory, as LOUIS
steps out onto the outer level with HUBERT ...

LOUIS

Yes sir ... Tell me about that park.

HUBERT

The park ... is amber ... Piles of freshly fallen
leaves cushion leaps from statues and trees. The sky
is that kind of blue that holds no threat of grey.
Cool autumn winds lick behind our ears, leaving
whispers of last summer— Remnants of sun-filled
hours.

HUBERT steps down onto the bottom surface level, and
moves downstage right ...

HUBERT

My mother— Laughing, throwing a gummy tennis
ball to our spaniel, Alfie. Grandma's egg
sandwiches, smothered in mustard, onions, and
poppy seeds. Grandpa's smoking pipe, infusing the
wind with a nutty aroma. This is paradise ...

The instrumental of "The Park Is Amber" softly fades.
HUBERT is drawn into gesture and movement during
the following.

HUBERT

Mother throws the ball several worlds away, and
Alfie and I run like two retrievers after the same
prey. Alfie gets there first. I wrestle him for the ball,
prying it from his jaws. I stand up, looking back at
my mother, holding the ball high in victory, to see
her violently slap my grandfather's cheek. My
grandmother bursts into tears. I know somehow
this fight can only be about me ... And my
paradise ... is lost.

Beat. HUBERT's up-stretched hand comes down to his side again ... Lighting changes ...

LOUIS

Paradise lost— I can relate to that.

HUBERT

Can you?

LOUIS leads HUBERT to the other side of the stage ...

LOUIS

My paradise— That would be Storyville, New Orleans man ...

The PIANO plays some New Orleans ragtime based on the "Prison Set Me Free" melody that holds through the following ...

LOUIS

... There's a great band playin' every night and I'm twelve— Runnin' round listenin' to them sounds ...

LOUIS crouches down and looks up at the TRUMPET PLAYER who stands up for a moment and plays a TRUMPET shot reminiscent of old New Orleans ... LOUIS stands up and continues ...

LOUIS

New Year's Eve! Biggest night of the year in New Orleans— People throwin' firecrackers and cherry bombs. Roman candles lightin' up the sky!

TRUMPET plays a lick sounding like a falling firework ...

LOUIS

And I felt I had to contribute somethin' to the festivities, so I borrowed my stepdaddy's thirty-eight, fully loaded, with blanks. I pointed that big

40

gun right at the sky, and fired. BANG, BANG, BANG, BANG!

> *PIANO out abruptly as LOUIS points his hand high in the air for his final "BANG!" …*

LOUIS

And these two massive white arms pinned me down …

> *LOUIS mimes being constrained by those arms, then …*

LOUIS

… Well they throw me in a bum wagon, and take me to the court house where I'm given an indeterminate sentence in the Colored Waif's Home. Jail … But that's where I got my first big chance, 'cause they had a band! And that's where I learned to play this horn. In jail. Yeah, that prison set me free!

> *PIANO in with "Prison Set Me Free." LOUIS mimes his trumpet as the TRUMPET PLAYER blows an intro …*

LOUIS

(*singing*) I once was a sinner
With no peace of mind
I rambled and gambled
In a sportin' life so blind
While locked in a prison
The good Lord came to me
Now I'm so happy
That prison set me free …
Praise the Lord
I'll meet you by and by
I'll be in Beulah Land
My cabin in the sky
I've thrown away my sportin' life
And that don't bother me

Praise the Lord
That prison set me free ...

LOUIS moves up into the inner hotel room, continuing to sing, and begins to jump up and down on the bed ...

Praise the Lord, that prison set me free ...
Praise the Lord, that prison set me free ...
Praise the Lord, that prison ...

Before the song is over, HUBERT interjects ...

HUBERT
Stop it! Stop it! Stop it!

PIANO out abruptly ... ...

LOUIS
These are sanctified sounds boy— Why you go stoppin' me like that?

HUBERT
I despise colloquial hymns of praise.

LOUIS
Oh yeah ... I guess you're more of a Mozart's Requiem kind of cat.

HUBERT
No, not really. I just think that the whole notion of getting a "Cabin in the Sky" is "Pie in the Sky."

LOUIS
Well I guess you was brought up heathen. Was you?

HUBERT
On the contrary ... Life with my father's parents. My other set of grandparents. They felt it was their duty to sanctify me in the blood of the lamb. So, I was treated daily with prayers of forgiveness, baptisms, evangelists, and tent-show revivals ...

The PIANO in with rain sounds under the following ...
HUBERT reacts to something falling on him from
above ...

LOUIS

What is it man?

HUBERT

It's raining.

LOUIS

Where?

HUBERT

In the tent, sinners all, grouped two by two ...

The musicians begin the instrumental tune
"Baptism," and it holds under the following ...

HUBERT

The rain collects in canvas gutters, pounding
polyphonic rhythms to the preacher's psalms of
damnation. The rolling of thunder! The calliope of
tongues! Me— Robed in linen, flanked by my
father's parents, walking, terrified, towards a huge
wooden rain barrel. I'm seated on the edge ...

HUBERT imitates a hellfire gospel preacher during the
following ... Instrumental continues under ...

HUBERT

And the preacher screams, "The sins of the father,
passed on to the son, most assuredly needs the
Holy Ghost! I said, The sins of the father, passed on
to the son, most assuredly needs the Holy Ghost!
Great God Almighty, grant your humble servant, I
said grant your humble servant, your divine power,
to wash those sins away! Can I get me an Amen? We
gonna baptize this boy! Can I get me an Amen?
Amen, and Amen, and A—"

The PIANO does one loud chord smear that slowly dies away under the following dialogue, as HUBERT is submerged underwater ... (Lighting change as well.)

HUBERT

Underwater— I wish for silence, but my heart pounds rage against the freezing water. Seconds feel like hours. How long will I be held under the surface? I let go of the breath I've been holding, and begin not to care ... I drift down, down into the sweet silent nothing. Thirteen years old, and I want to die ...

HUBERT curls up on his knees, taking on the fetal position. LOUIS helps him to his feet, and leads him to the other side of the downstage area ...

LOUIS

Now don't go drownin' in self pity Eubie. There's a million ways of playin' your line ...

LOUIS plays the Bach lick on the TRUMPET, once again à la jazz, but with a bit more feeling and expression this time ...

HUBERT

But only one way is the right way.

HUBERT moves back up to the inner hotel room. LOUIS follows ...

LOUIS

You know something? You're right. But obviously you don't know what that is.

HUBERT

Oh, and I suppose you do.

LOUIS

Sure I do. Love to tell ya'! All you got to do is ask.

HUBERT

Ask? You and I both know a team of wild horses
couldn't *stop* you from telling me.

LOUIS

No baby, it would take a team of elephants! Huh,
huh, huh.

HUBERT

Okay then Louis. I'm asking. What's the right way?

LOUIS

Your way Hubert, your way! Be original. Genuine.
The real McCoy!

HUBERT

I'm original. I'm genuine!

LOUIS

Oh yeah, you're genuine all right. So genuine that
you blame all your troubles on everybody else. Like
me, like Volkovsky, like your grandparents, and
even your own mother. Are you sure you never dug
ditches before?

HUBERT

Why?

LOUIS

'Cause you're certainly shovelling it now! Oh
Eubie! I can understand why your wife is thinking
of leaving you.

HUBERT

This is not about my wife. This is about the Bach
passage!

LOUIS

You're not playing that either, are you? And you
know why? You're bitter. Brittle, ironic, always so
chilly. Why you so chilly Hubert?

HUBERT gets ready at the cello. The PIANO plays the single note melody of the passage, while HUBERT stares at the score.

At the ready, HUBERT mimes playing the passage along with the CELLIST, and messes it up again. He leans back on the chair in a blue funk.

LOUIS

Where are you man? You're a million miles from that passage.

HUBERT is drawn into a memory ...

HUBERT

Montreal.

LOUIS

Montreal! Love that town. Used to come up there just for jam sessions. What are you doing there?

HUBERT

Living, with my mother ...

LOUIS

Your mother ... Good. Now maybe we're getting somewhere. Tell it.

HUBERT

She's working nights as a waitress. She buys me a new cello, from tips she's saved in a big Mason jar ...

LOUIS

You must feel like a million dollars.

HUBERT remembers old feelings ...

HUBERT

What I feel is a deep responsibility to her, to advance further with my cello.

LOUIS

Oh yeah, she gives you love, and you turn it into a contractual agreement.

HUBERT

It is a contractual agreement. Life is hard for her— She's a single white mother and she always has to explain me being black.

LOUIS

She's the cream in your coffee!

HUBERT

I have a regimented practice schedule, that she helps me organize. Every night, after supper.

LOUIS

Montreal ...

> *PIANO in and under on intro/vamp to "King of the Night" a shew-op type melody with a fifties jazz/hip feel ...*

> *LOUIS crosses down to the lower level, next to the musicians, as the lights change, building an ambience ...*

LOUIS

New Orleans North!

> *TRUMPET plays a sultry muted line ...*

LOUIS

Now that's a party town.

> *TRUMPET plays a rising muted line ... LOUIS looks back at HUBERT ...*

LOUIS

You mean to tell me that every night you just stayed in and sawed on that cello baby?

> *HUBERT thinks, looking around ...*

HUBERT
No …

*TRUMPET plays a slightly suspenseful line, as
HUBERT considers his escape …*

HUBERT
Like most teenagers faced with this kind of
regimen … I secretly make my escape from time to
time.

*HUBERT mimes opening a window in his room, and
surreptitiously makes his escape through the window,
out onto the outer level …*

LOUIS
Oh yeah, you got to get out right? To commune
with your amigos!

*Lighting change … A streetlight … The outer level
becomes a street corner …*

HUBERT
Light— Streaming down through darkness, from a
street lamp …

TRUMPET plays another sultry muted line …

HUBERT
It's late Friday night, hot summer night.

TRUMPET plays yet another sultry line …

HUBERT
Harmonies from young black voices embrace the
sidewalks. Four brothers in song. A bottle of wine
passes from hand to hand …

*TRUMPET plays another line as HUBERT mimes being
given and drinking from a bottle of wine …*

HUBERT
… Providing back-up to this soulful "a cappella."

> *PIANO picks up the tempo ... HUBERT mimes being asked to sing by the brothers, and refusing shyly ...*

LOUIS

Sing it Eubie!

> *HUBERT mimes being seemingly propelled forward by the brothers. He begins to sing, self-consciously at first ...*

HUBERT

(*sings*) King of the night
Feelin' so right
Underneath the moon
Melody
Harmony
Rhyming a rhythm of love
Darling don't be shy
I won't make you cry
And when we're all alone
Hold me tight
Treat me right
And I'll be your king of the night

LOUIS

(*scats*) Ba do bad ba da ta too to tway ...

> *HUBERT looks up ...*

HUBERT

(*spoken*) Young women watch and listen from windowsills and doorsteps, swaying to each and every cadence we produce ...

> *TRUMPET plays a line reminiscent of the swaying ...*

HUBERT

(*spoken*) We are kings of the night!

LOUIS

(*laughs*) One more Eubie, one more!

(second verse) HUBERT begins to dance, and directs his singing to the windowsills …

HUBERT

(*sings*) Turn down the lights
It would be so right
Let your heart run free
You and me
Tenderly
Wrapped up in a blanket of love
Darling it's so true
That my love for you
Is deep inside my heart
Hold me tight
Treat me right
And I'll be your king of the night

    (*bridge*)

Wanting
Gentle whispers in my ear
Secrets of the night
Hearing
You say soft in my ears
Words that go straight to my heart

HUBERT makes a heart shape with his hands for the benefit of the women in the windowsills … He begins to dance more confidently …

HUBERT

(*soulfully singing*) King of the night

LOUIS

(*scats a response*)

HUBERT

(*sings*) Feelin' so right

LOUIS

(*scats a response*)

HUBERT

(*sings*) Underneath the moon

Melody

Harmony

Rhyming a rhythm of love

Darling don't be shy

I won't make you cry

And when we're all alone

Hold me tight

Treat me right

And I'll be your king ...

LOUIS

(*answering*) I'll be your king.

HUBERT

(*sings*) I'll be your king ...

LOUIS

(*answering*) I'll be your king.

HUBERT

(*sings*) I'll be your king ...

> PIANO drops out ... HUBERT sings the next line
> a cappella ...

HUBERT

(*drawn out/very soulfully singing*) Of the night ...

> A big ending ... The PIANO slips back in, vamping the
> tune under the following ...

HUBERT

(*spoken*) It's Alfonse's turn to take the lead ... But instead, he taps my arm, and says to someone behind me, "Hey pretty lady, are you lost, can I help?" I turn, slowly, drafting an even sweeter offer, only to see ...

PIANO music out abruptly. An empty spotlight comes up on the lower level, downstage right …

HUBERT

My mother … Standing there, with a look of sheer dismay and disappointment on her face. She looks deep into my eyes, seeking recognition. I'm in no hurry to claim ownership. I turn back quickly to the brothers. I look back towards my mother. She stands there, growing roots into the sidewalk.

HUBERT looks back and forth between the positions of his mother and the brothers, caught between these two points.

HUBERT

Alfonse sizes up my mother. He says, "Isn't it a little *dark* for you to be down here this time of night? Maybe you need a chaperone." My mother gestures to me to come with her. Alfonse turns to me, "Hey, Eubie, ain't you the lucky boy," then he looks at my mother. "Hey, what's wrong with my action?" he says. And I say, "Cool it Alfonse … She's my mom."

Beat.

HUBERT

The brothers examine the differences between me, and my mother. My position with this group has now suddenly and irrevocably changed. Mom says, "Hubert, it's time to come home." I stand there, not moving a muscle. Alfonse says, "What's the matter Eubie, past your bedtime?" I say nothing. Mom's eyes fill with tears. She turns, and runs away into the night.

HUBERT turns back to the brothers, as the empty spotlight fades where his mom was standing.

HUBERT

Alfonse asks, "Hey man, are you adopted?" I think about my options, then reply, "No." The brothers exchange glances, but not with me. And though minutes ago our voices sang in harmony, my voice once again sings alone.

HUBERT runs downstage right, as if catching up to someone, as the spotlight comes on again.

HUBERT

I run, and catch up with Mom. She's happy to see me. We don't discuss what just happened. We both know.

LOUIS crosses to HUBERT.

LOUIS

What did you both know Eubie? That those boys were gonna cut you out of their scene because of your mother? What was it Eubie?

Beat. HUBERT doesn't answer, and LOUIS leads HUBERT to the other side of the stage ...

LOUIS

Okay Eubie, now when's the last time you saw your momma?

HUBERT props his chin in his hand, and ponders for a moment ...

HUBERT

It's been a while, not since my college days.

LOUIS

Oh yes of course, your college days!!! Tell me, "Professor," did you connect with her?

HUBERT is drawn into a memory ...

HUBERT

My mother had remarried ...

53

Music in, and holds under, on the instrumental tune
"Walking Through My Mother's Hood."

HUBERT

It's Easter break, and guess who gets invited to
dinner. (*little laugh*).

He walks, as if smelling something on the air, as the
lighting changes … LOUIS follows HUBERT around
the perimeter of the outer level …

LOUIS

What is it Eubie?

HUBERT

The ambrosia of freshly cut lawns, each blade of
grass manicured to perfection … I'm walking
through Mother's new neighbourhood. It's
evening, and in the failing light, my eyes strain to
make out the numbers on the houses— Every
house is exactly the same.

Puzzled, HUBERT looks at three or four of the identical
houses. (Lighting: shafts of light.)

HUBERT

I become aware of triangular shafts of light—
Curtains being drawn and peeked through before
being quickly shut again. I imagine what might be
said behind each curtain.

LOUIS

Like what?

HUBERT

Is he lost? Is he on delivery? What is he doing here?

LOUIS

(*chuckles*) You're a stranger in a strange land …

HUBERT

Exactly …

HUBERT spots his "mother's house" and walks towards it.

HUBERT

I make my way to my mother's doorstep, and knock.

Music out as HUBERT knocks …

HUBERT

Mother opens the door, and we embrace. The triangles of light open and close one last time. I meet her new husband. He's a nice man. "Hubert, nice to meet you! We hope you like lamb!" I meet his children from a previous marriage. They're all very nice people. We make friendly conversation.

HUBERT remembers the dinner more clearly …

HUBERT

The mint sauce really complements the meat. (*beat*) The mustard very much complements the mint sauce! (*beat*) Mother asks me if I would like another bread roll … I take one and break it open. I look into the white bread. I begin to feel like I'm falling headlong into it …

HUBERT physicalizes the following …

HUBERT

I find myself rising from the table, grabbing my coat, thanking them for their hospitality, and running out the door … In the yard, my mother catches up to me. She physically stops me, and spins me around.

HUBERT is swung around …

HUBERT

We're finally looking eye to eye. I say, "If that's what you wanted out of life, why did you marry my

father? Why did you marry him in the first place?"
Mother replies simply, "I loved him." She leans
forward ...

> *HUBERT "holds" his mother's shoulders ...*

HUBERT
> I kiss her goodnight, and withdraw ... But Mom
> holds on tightly to my arms, slowing my retreat.
> She holds me, still. Her eyes fill with love,
> understanding, and concern. She says, "I have a
> loving family now, but I will always love you, and I
> will always love your father."

> *Beat.*

HUBERT
> But my father was dead. How could she love a dead
> man?

LOUIS
> So, it's your mom that's stopping you from playin'
> that Bach passage.

HUBERT
> (*considers*) No ... That's not it.

> *HUBERT isn't ready to confront where his mind is
> leading, and moves quickly back into the inner room to
> his music stand ...*

HUBERT
> Stupid, stupid, stupid! I've got to attack the passage
> systematically.

> *The PIANO plays the single notes of the Bach
> passage ...*

> *HUBERT plays the Bach line, and blows it again.*

HUBERT
> My problem is purely technical. It's my phrasing!

LOUIS

Phrasing, my man, phrasing! Okay … Yeah …
Phrasing … The riff, the ramble, the jelly roll …

HUBERT

By "riff," I suppose you mean the passage?

LOUIS

Correct Professor. And secondly, the ramble!

HUBERT

I presume you're talking about rhythm.

LOUIS

You are a quick study. Ain't no flies on you! And
finally there's the jelly roll!

HUBERT

I'm aware of the sexual connotations of the term
"jelly roll," but in this context I'm assuming you're
referring to "expression" and "feeling."

LOUIS

Whatever you say! (*beat*)

Now in phrasing, and in life Eubie, the rests are
just as vital as the notes.

HUBERT

I'll give you that.

LOUIS

Okay, for your benefit, and 'cause you'd
understand it better, let's see what the textbooks
say about it. Mmmmme …

> *LOUIS rifles through an imaginary textbook, and does
> the next quote in his own version of an English accent.*

LOUIS

"Phrasing is the ability of the performer to give
personal meaning to a musical line." Hah hah hah
hah … Now listen to this …

TRUMPET/PIANO intro: LOUIS "lifts his trumpet" and mimes playing the solo intro of "Down in New Orleans" along with the TRUMPET PLAYER and the PIANO … After the solo, the piano continues vamping the tune …

LOUIS

That was how I used to play it, when I was just startin' out in New Orleans. I'm giggin' for baptisms, weddings, some great funerals, and even a few Bar Mitzvahs! …

PIANO vamp out abruptly as HUBERT interjects …

HUBERT

That's all well and good Louis. You're a kid, playing in whorehouses and on the street! But I'm principal cellist of a major orchestra! What can you possibly tell me that would change my situation tonight?

LOUIS

If you permit me to finish my thought, I'll tell you about the day I got a call from the King himself! King Joe Oliver, and he asks me to join his band! He's the hottest cornet player in the jazz world!

HUBERT

Why am I sitting here talking to Louis Armstrong? I'm losing my mind!

LOUIS crosses up to the bathroom mirror …

LOUIS

You know perfectly well why I'm here. You're the one who brought me out of this mirror my friend …

HUBERT looks to his music stand, then back to LOUIS.

HUBERT

Okay fine— New Orleans— Joe Oliver. What about him?

*PIANO vamp back in. "Down in New Orleans"—
LOUIS laughs, and leads HUBERT to the downstage
left lower level, next to the PIANO PLAYER and the
TRUMPET PLAYER ...*

LOUIS

Old one-eyed Joe Oliver! He's the kind of guy who could sit down, eat three whole chickens, then top it off with two apple pies and a quart of ice cream! He teaches me a lot. I'm tryin' to get his style down.

*TRUMPET line: LOUIS mimes as the TRUMPET
PLAYER plays the first head line of "Down in New
Orleans" ...*

LOUIS

He sees me studying his fingers every night. And one night, after I've played three consecutive solos using exactly the same notes as Joe, he figures he's gonna fix my wagon, and he brings out this big old handkerchief ...

*LOUIS produces his large white handkerchief, and cov-
ers his left hand with it. The handkerchief comes to
represent Joe Oliver's trumpet.*

LOUIS

... Covering up his fingers so I can't see 'em, you understand. He looks at me as if to say, "Follow this sucker," then he blows his first line ...

*The TRUMPET PLAYER blows Joe's lead line, as LOUIS
manipulates the handkerchief like a puppet ...*

LOUIS

Man, I gotta use my ears now, 'cause I can't see that
bastard's fingers. I figure I'm gonna counter with
an idea I've been workin' on— Half-valvin', just to
give him somethin' to think about for a change ...

> *LOUIS mimes playing with his trumpet in his right
> hand, as the TRUMPET PLAYER plays his line, which
> counters Joe's line. This line incorporates the half-valve
> technique, creating a whole new level of trumpet
> complexity ... (LOUIS' left hand is still covered with the
> handkerchief ...)*

LOUIS

I'm thinkin', I got him now! But then, he changes
up on me, dividing each beat, four to one! Like
this ...

> *The TRUMPET PLAYER blows Joe's line, doubling the
> rhythm ... LOUIS keeps looking at the handkerchief in
> his left hand. The "wind" of Joe's line flutters through
> the handkerchief.*

LOUIS

Joe's leavin' me no room for error! He's squeezin'
me like *I'm* a half-valved note! He's pushing me up
against the wall! I've got one more ace in my bag of
tricks, but I got to reach right up into the sky to
pull it out! Like this ...

> *LOUIS mimes countering Joe's line with a flurry of
> notes, culminating in a finish on E-flat, above high C.
> This is one scorching high note that the TRUMPET
> PLAYER plays and holds for a long, long, long, time!!!
> When it's over ...*

LOUIS

Old Joe looks back at me, squeezin' more evil out
of that one eye of his, than the devil could with his

two! He lifts his horn high in the air, like he's
gonna blow even higher ...

> *LOUIS elevates the handkerchief even higher in the air*
> *as the TRUMPET PLAYER points his trumpet even*
> *higher towards the sky ...*

LOUIS

... But he stops ... And the big man walks over to
me. He takes that handkerchief from around his
horn, and gently drapes it over mine.

> *LOUIS moves the handkerchief from his left hand to his*
> *right hand ...*

LOUIS

He says, "I guess you learned all I could teach you."
I take that handkerchief off my horn, and mop my
brow with it. And ever since that day, I always use a
handkerchief when I play my horn.

> *The PIANO in on the tune a little louder, as LOUIS*
> *finally sings "Down in New Orleans" with great spirit!*

LOUIS

(*singing*) There's a club down in New Orleans
Where everyone will be your best friend
Don't matter if you're dark or light
The good times never end
Come down and see us
We'll give you a smile
We're glad to see ya'
So stay for a while
We'll all have a wonderful time
Down in New Orleans

    (*second verse*)

Take a trip on a riverboat
Steamin' down to old New Orleans

Steamboat captain can be heard to shout
"Here comes the land of dreams!"
Come down and see us
We'll give you a smile
We're glad to see ya'
So stay for a while
We'll all have a wonderful time
Down in New Orleans

> *(bridge)*

The land of dreams
Is what it means

Party 'til the break of day
And when that sun comes up
We'll start all over again
> *(Repeat first verse, then ...)*

Down in New Orleans
Down in New Orleans

LOUIS
> *(spoken)* I really mean it!

> *The number cooks to a climax and finishes with a
> scorching TRUMPET solo. LOUIS mops his brow with
> his handkerchief ...*

LOUIS
> Old Joe Oliver, he was just like a father to me ...

> *LOUIS runs back upstage to the inner hotel room ...*

LOUIS
> Hey Eubie, maybe we oughta check out this here
> mini-bar! What do you say?

HUBERT
> Keep out of that mini-bar! I have a concert tonight,
> and I still haven't made my Bach passage work!

> *HUBERT crosses towards the music stand ...*

LOUIS

Oh yeah, almost forgot. We talked about phrasing,
now baby we got to talk about emotional content!
Feeling Eubie! Yeah … Feeling. If you don't live it,
it don't come out your horn …

HUBERT

I don't have time Louis!

LOUIS

We already know that from the way you're playin'
that Bach passage.

HUBERT

(*dryly*) Ha, ha.

LOUIS

Feeling Eubie. If you don't feel it, you can't squeal
it. You got to deal with feeling! Or there ain't no
expression in your song my man. No amount of
finger exercises are gonna change that. You don't
believe me? Go ahead, try it then.

HUBERT

All right. I will.

> The PIANO plays the melody of the Bach passage, as
> HUBERT psyches himself up to play his entry …
> HUBERT picks up his "cello" and his "bow" …
>
> HUBERT plays the passage, and blows it completely. It's
> the worst it's been so far.
>
> Frustrated, HUBERT gets up, grabs the Bach score from
> his music stand, and throws the pages high in the air!

HUBERT

(*screams*) Ahhhhh!!!

> The music pages of the score flutter and land all over
> the stage, as HUBERT collapses on the bed.

LOUIS
> Exactly Hubert. You're lookin' for feeling baby, not for those dots on them pages!

> *LOUIS moves to HUBERT ...*

LOUIS
> Come on Eubie! Tell me about your daddy!

HUBERT
> (*turns around*) I don't feel like talking about my father.

LOUIS
> Play the lick Eubie! Play the riff! Play your truth!

> *The musicians begin the instrumental "Sydney–Montreal Run," and hold under ... HUBERT stands up, drawn into a memory ...*

HUBERT
> My father was a great man ... He takes me on his train when I'm five years old. He's a porter on the Sydney–Montreal run. I love his uniform. It's blue, with yellow piping, and his cap gives him the demeanour of a rear admiral! He marches through the train to announce the stops ...

> *HUBERT moves to the downstage right lower level as he imitates his father ...*

HUBERT
> "Next stop— Antigonish! The highland heart of Nova Scotia! Unfortunately, I left my kilt at home!"

> *Music out. LOUIS laughs ...*

HUBERT
> He had a humorous anecdote for every stop along the way. He shows me the whole train, and tells me how everything works. I'm so proud of him!

> *HUBERT remembers his father ... LOUIS interjects ...*

LOUIS

Family! The only thing we got in this world!

HUBERT

What do you know about family Louis? You never had any kids.

LOUIS

I was never lucky enough to have two little ice-cream-eaters at home like you do, but all the little children that were ever around me, always called me "Pops."

HUBERT

(*sarcastic*) Okay "Pops." And I suppose "It's a wonderful world," and "The whole wonderful world is one big happy family"!

LOUIS

It could be ...

> *PIANO in. LOUIS sings "The Storm to the Rainbow."*

LOUIS

(*sings*) The world could be
A heaven here on earth
Filled with bright and shiny days
But in our time
There's so much pain and sorrow
How can we live another day?

> *(B part)*

How to get through the storm to the rainbow
When the wind
Won't let you make your way
Deep in your heart
You search for tomorrow
'Til you find your bright and shiny day

> *(second verse)*

When all seems lost
When you're torn and weary
There is no road that you can take
There's no way out
That you can beg or borrow
When will sadness ever break?

(B part)

How to get through the storm to the rainbow
When the wind
Won't let you make your way
Deep in your heart
You search for tomorrow
'Til you find your bright and shiny day

> *TRUMPET solo: Instrumental on the tune of the*
> *verse … Followed by reprise of B part, sung …*

LOUIS

(*sings*) How to get through the storm to the
rainbow
When the wind
Won't let you make your way
Deep in your heart
You search for tomorrow
'Til you find your bright and shiny day

> *The tune finishes …*

HUBERT

Thank you Louis. That was lovely. So basically
you're telling me that the more misery I go
through sooner or later things will get better.

LOUIS

Oh Eubie, you still don't get it do you? The way I
see it, people go through all the troubles of this
world for one thing, and that's their family.

HUBERT

What do you know about family "Pops"? You never had your own. And your mother was a good time girl in Storyville, and your father didn't even believe you were his son! I've heard all about you Louis!

LOUIS

How come you know so much about me, and you know so little about yourself Eubie?

LOUIS looks at the sheet music scattered on the floor, then continues ...

LOUIS

I know why you're havin' trouble with that Bach lick. You're all beaten up inside! And whatever it is, you're not facing it. Face it, my man, or you're never gonna play that lick! Winter skies ... Winter skies man ...

Beat.

HUBERT reluctantly looks up at the sky, as if examining something.

HUBERT

Winter skies— Grey, too cold for wind ...

LOUIS

How old are you?

HUBERT

I'm eight years old.

LOUIS

Where you livin' now?

HUBERT

Our family lives in Montreal.

LOUIS

Where's your momma?

HUBERT

> My mother leaves to care for my grandparents back on the East Coast. They're both very ill, I'm told.

LOUIS

> Yeah, it's just you and your daddy.

HUBERT

> Dad and I become bachelors. He phones in sick, and cancels his train runs, just so he can stay home with me!
>
> > *HUBERT smiles for a second ...*

HUBERT

> He lets me stay up late.
>
> > *HUBERT looks at LOUIS, remembering and realizing ...*

HUBERT

> We listen to Louis Armstrong records ... My father knows all the tunes. He dusts each record carefully with a special cloth, anointing them, before putting them on the turntable ... He loved you Satchmo'.

LOUIS

> Yeah ...

HUBERT

> For my father, your life and work represents an attitude towards life that makes it worth living.

LOUIS

> A wonderful world ...
>
> > *Beat.*

HUBERT

> Yes that's right. And for a while, it's a great adventure staying up late, listening to your music. But soon, we both begin to yearn for my mom. The

more Dad tries to seem strong and in control, the more I sense his longing.

In the recounting of the story, HUBERT squirms a little …

HUBERT

As weeks become months, he doesn't sleep at all. He doesn't eat. He begins to waste away. I become our cook and try to get him to eat. I know he doesn't swallow— Though sometimes he pretends to. He doesn't bother to phone in sick anymore. He simply doesn't go. Late into the night, we listen to you singing "What a Wonderful World" over and over again.

LOUIS

But it ain't so wonderful, is it?

HUBERT

No.

LOUIS

So what happens man?

It gets harder and harder for HUBERT to face this, but he continues …

HUBERT

I begin to realize Mother isn't coming back. My grandparents have somehow convinced her, to leave my father, and me, because … because …

LOUIS

Because of what Hubert?

HUBERT

Every time I think of this, it fills me with rage!

LOUIS

Tell it!

HUBERT
> My mother chooses to listen to my grandparent's
> ignorant prejudice, for what? So that they can sleep
> better at night knowing that their daughter isn't
> with "that coloured boy." They make my family
> extinct, and for what? It didn't have to happen!
> There was no good reason for it. It's a huge ugly
> mistake!
>
> > *HUBERT is getting closer to the part of the story that he
> > really wants to avoid, but he continues, setting a chair
> > in the middle of the room representing his father. He
> > kneels beside it …*

HUBERT
> My father talks endlessly of his love for my mother,
> through a kind of continuous night. Her beauty.
> Her softness, her love for me.
>
> > *HUBERT takes a big beat. LOUIS presses him further,
> > kneeling on the other side of the chair.*

LOUIS
> What is it Eubie? Come on!

HUBERT
> You know what it is Louis.

LOUIS
> Yeah, I know Eubie … (*Beat. He stands up.*) A job I
> had one time down in Tennessee! … Man the place
> was packed …
>
> > *PIANO starts vamping the tune "Life Is What You
> > Make It," and holds under …*

LOUIS
> People from everywhere. Black and white. Yes, an
> integrated crowd.
>
> > *LOUIS sits HUBERT in his chair …*

70

LOUIS

Why don't you play that undersized bass fiddle of
yours?

> *HUBERT "bows" a bass line on the cello along with the*
> *vamp. It's a bit stiff.*

LOUIS

Swing it Eubie! Eight to the bar!

> *The CELLO picks up with a bit of swing, plucking the*
> *strings.*

LOUIS

That's it. You're ready now! Man the music is just
simmerin', and in the second set, we started to
boil! When up comes my verse ...

LOUIS

(*sings*) Life is what you make it
We've heard the wise men say
One day you're eatin' caviar
The next you're eatin' hay
So what are you gonna do
When you can't seize the day
Just remember that the golden ring
Is just a reach away ...

> *The PIANO continues under for the first eight bars of*
> *the piece as ...*

LOUIS

(*spoken*) I point my horn towards the sky ...

> *TRUMPET line: LOUIS points his horn at the sky and*
> *"plays" a trumpet lick with the tune ...*

LOUIS

(*spoken*) Then I come down to give the crowd some.

*TRUMPET line: Pointing his horn down, LOUIS
"plays" another lick miming with the TRUMPET
PLAYER ...*

LOUIS

(*sings*) Keep your eyes on the prize
Don't let it slip away
And though you've got troubles now
Tomorrow's a better day ...

The music continues under ...

LOUIS

(*spoken*) Everybody's havin' a wonderful time! And
then, BOOM!!!

*All musicians play a loud chord smear. LOUIS is
thrown a couple of steps, and all feel the force of the
blast ...*

LOUIS

The biggest damn explosion since D-Day! That
theatre was practically knocked right off its
foundation. Some fine folks wearing bed sheets
decided that the mix of people I'm entertaining
don't belong in the same room. They're trying to
blow us apart with a bomb. A real bomb Hubert,
not a little insult.

LOUIS moves downstage to the lower level.

LOUIS

People are terrorized out of their minds. I look to
see if anyone's hurt. And the family's doin' fine! So
I say, "Everything's all right ladies and gents, it's
just my telephone ringin' again." And I don't know
if it was me ...

PIANO vamp of "Life Is What You Make It" back in ...

LOUIS

... The music, the bomb, or the fear, but everybody breaks up laughin'! We's ALIVE!!!

And then the band gets louder!

> *TRUMPET line as LOUIS walks back upstage and gets on the outer level ...*

LOUIS

(*sings*) Life hands you a moment
Every second of the day
You can choose to take it
Or you can throw it away
You can walk on a sunny street
Or walk in shades of grey
The choice is yours so make it friend
I hope you find your way.

> *TRUMPET line: LOUIS blows an ending along with the TRUMPET PLAYER.*

LOUIS

Oh yeah!

HUBERT

Just what are you trying to tell me Louis?

LOUIS

Eubie, you're the white audience, you're the black audience, and you're standing in that theatre! Now where you goin' to direct your feet my man?

> *HUBERT looks up towards the sky ...*

HUBERT

Winter skies— Grey, too cold for wind ...

LOUIS

You walk home from school ...

HUBERT

> I climb the wooden stairs leading up to our
> apartment. They groan and bend with each step I
> take towards our door ... The air ...

LOUIS

> Thinner than usual ...

HUBERT

> Wafts uneasily down the staircase ... Gas ...

LOUIS

> You don't want to open that door ...

HUBERT

> But no one else will ...

> > *HUBERT opens an imaginary door and enters. LOUIS
> > follows behind him ...*

HUBERT

> The shades are drawn. The hiss of gas. I move to
> the kitchen ... My father. His feet, bent over. His
> knees, press into the floor. A rope under his
> shoulders, and tied to the grate, holds his body
> inside the oven. His hands clutch the door like
> supplicants at confession. But his soul has gone ...

> > *An emotional beat for HUBERT. Tears roll down his
> > cheeks.*

> > *A CELLO drone note marks the opening
> > accompaniment of "The Skin I'm In."*

> > *LOUIS sings the first verse over the drone ...*

LOUIS

> (*singing*) Can't hide
> It's plain to see
> People laugh— Scornin' me
> Acting like it's a sin
> All because of the skin I'm in ...

(second verse) PIANO *joins arrangement* ...

LOUIS

(singing) No ground
On which to stand
People don't— Understand
There's no way I can win
All because of the skin I'm in ...

LOUIS

(spoken) You want some of this?

     HUBERT takes the chorus ...

HUBERT

(sings) Outside I'm smiling
It makes such a brave masquerade
Inside I'm dying
'Cause I know that my mask's a charade ...

(sings verse) No ground
On which to stand
People don't— Understand
There's no way I can win
All because of the skin I'm in ...

LOUIS

(background vocal) ... Oh yeah ...

     LOUIS scats through next chorus ...

HUBERT

(sings chorus) Outside I'm smiling
It makes such a brave masquerade
Inside I'm dying
'Cause I know that my mask's a charade ...

LOUIS

(sings) No lies

HUBERT

(sings) Got to just be

LOUIS
(*sings*) Someone real truly free

HUBERT
(*sings*) We all know there's no sin

LOUIS
(*sings*) Makes no difference the skin I'm in …

HUBERT
(*sings*) Makes no difference the skin I'm in …

LOUIS & HUBERT
(*singing together*) Makes no difference the skin I'm …

HUBERT
(*sings a cappella*) In …

The song ends.

LOUIS
Atta boy Eubie … Took a lot of courage to face that. I'm proud of you.

HUBERT
Thanks.

LOUIS
You let it out! You let it all out! There's blue skies for you man, from now on …

HUBERT
You think so?

LOUIS
Believe it man. Just believe it …

HUBERT
I apologize for all the insulting names I called you.

LOUIS

Hey, don't worry about it … We both know you never believed any of that … Old Pops just wants you to be happy. Huh, huh, huh …

LOUIS produces his handkerchief …

LOUIS

You know Eubie, I think you should hang on to this here handkerchief for a while …

LOUIS passes the handkerchief to HUBERT.

HUBERT

(*respectfully*) Are you sure King Oliver would approve?

LOUIS

I'm sure he'd be pleased. You've learned all I have to teach you. You give that passage another shot. The rest is up to you.

The phone on stage rings. Lighting changes as HUBERT races towards the phone and picks it up …

HUBERT

(*into phone*) Rosie? … Ahhh! Thanks for calling back.

HUBERT tries to pull himself together …

HUBERT

I've been thinking about us all day … You? … You're the sweetest … And you know what they say, the blacker the berry, the sweeter the juice …

HUBERT looks around to share this last line with LOUIS, but LOUIS is gone …

Carrying the phone, HUBERT crosses right …

HUBERT

Rosie ... I was thinking ... When I get home ...
You and me and the boys could go and visit my
mother ... What do you say? You still with me?

*He anxiously waits for her answer, hears it and jumps
with joy, then says quietly ...*

HUBERT

Thanks ...

He smiles, relieved ...

HUBERT

Volkovsky? Oh yeah, he made a stupid remark
about Louis Armstrong ... Comparing me to him,
you know?

HUBERT reflects ...

HUBERT

Hey, I've decided, I'm gonna take his remark as a
compliment ...

HUBERT tenses ...

HUBERT

The Bach passage? Right!

HUBERT checks his wristwatch ...

HUBERT

I gotta run, I'm playing in an hour. I've got to get it
right, just once! ... I love you.

HUBERT hangs up ...

*PIANO, CELLO, and TRUMPET make sounds of an
orchestra tuning up with a long tuning note that holds
under the following ...*

*HUBERT picks up his "cello," walks out of the inner
room, and crosses down to the lower level ... When he*

*gets there, he nods to other "members of the orchestra"
as the tuning note continues ...*

*HUBERT sits down centre stage, and "bows" the
tuning note on his "cello," tuning along with the other
musicians ...*

*The TRUMPET PLAYER makes the sound of "Tap, Tap,
Tap, Tap, Tap" (the conductor's baton) by tapping on
his music stand.*

The tuning note stops.

*HUBERT looks up at the conductor, and then begins to
play the piece. As the passage we have heard him
continually flub approaches, the lights fade down
to ... A thin intense spotlight on HUBERT "playing"
his cello ...*

HUBERT plays the passage beautifully ...

*HUBERT finishes the prelude with energy, precision,
and strength.*

Blackout.

The End.

DATE DUE	RETURNED